THE COMPLETE GUIDE TO
MARKETING SUCCESS FOR LANDSCAPERS

Christopher Yates

This publication is licensed to the individual reader only. Duplication or distribution by any means, including email, disk, photocopy and recording, to a person other than the original purchaser is a violation of international copyright law.

Publisher: Visual Success Marketing
1133 Louisiana Ave. Suite 100, Winter Park, FL 32789

While they have made every effort to verify the information here, neither the author nor the publisher assumes any responsibility of errors in, omissions from or different interpretation of the subject matter. This information may be subject to varying laws and businesses in different areas, states and countries. The reader assumes all responsibility for use of the information.

The author and publisher shall in no event be held liable to any party for any damages arising directly or indirectly from any use of this material. Every effort has been made to accurately represent this information and there is no guarantee that you will earn money using these techniques.

Copyright © 2016

Christopher Yates

All rights reserved.

ISBN-13: 978-1537575599
ISBN-10:1537575597

DEDICATION

This book is dedicated to my beautiful wife, Beverly, who has been my best friend and constant encouragement for over thirty years.

The life of an entrepreneur certainly has times of victory as well as its share of challenges, and through it all, I have been incredibly blessed to always have her by my side. I love you, Bev!

"It's kind of fun to do the impossible."
Walt Disney

Visit our website:
http://www.successlandscapemarketing.com
for more marketing tips, ideas and resources.

Table of Contents
Chapter 1
Your Brand and Your Marketing..........................7

Chapter 2 Direct Mail: Friend or Foe?.............................11

Chapter 3 Harnessing The Power of The Internet.............19

    Google My Business..20

    Getting Google+ And Other Reviews................................22

    Our System For Reputation Management.......................23

    The Importance of Citations for Your Business...............25

    Optimizing Your Web Site...29

    Your Complete Website Checklist....................................32

    Pay-Per-Click Advertising..50

Chapter 4 Social Media Strategies....................................59

    Getting Started on Twitter..60

    Maximizing Facebook For Your Busines.........................66

    Using YouTube to Market Your Business........................79

Chapter 5 Developing an Email Marketing Strategy.........87

Email Marketing Dictionary..94

Chapter 6 Staying on Top of Landscaping Trends...........105

Chapter 7 Next Steps: Developing Your Plan of Action..107

"I think we need to raise awareness, explain the benefits ... and if that doesn't work, just bite 'em."

CHAPTER 1
Your Brand and Your Marketing

One of the many nostalgic memories I remember from my childhood is driving out with my Dad to "Pop Pop's" barn. There was always something magical about seeing the big barn door being pushed open as I anticipated going inside. A small window in the back of the barn allowed sunlight to stream as Pop Pop would fiddle with turning on the lights. The lights quickly came on and my eyes would jump from place to place as I looked at all of the treasures stored in the barn.

On one of our visits I remember asking my Dad about something that had caught my attention, hanging on the side of the barn. My Dad explained to me that it was called a branding iron. It was used to brand Pop Pop's cattle which enabled the cattle to easily be identified. No one else had the same design, so his cattle stood apart from the others.

Branding for your business is very much the same idea. It is defined as, "The marketing practice of creating a name, symbol or design that identifies and differentiates one product from other products."

I have often heard a business owner use the words "branding" and "marketing" interchangeably, as if they meant the same thing. There is a difference. Branding goes deeper than your marketing. Your brand is made up of your voice, your personality and the message that you want to convey. The foundation of your brand is your logo. Your website, your trucks, your business cards, and your promotional materials all should contain your logo, which communicates your brand.

Branding is a strategic action, while marketing is tactical. Marketing is the various channels that are used to promote your business. Some examples are your website, direct mail, PPC, social media, etc. Branding is the message that permeates your business.

Marketing says "Buy Me" or "You need this service" while branding will help encourage someone to purchase. It says, "This is what I am, this is why I exist."

Marketing may contribute to a brand, but the brand is bigger than any particular marketing method or campaign. The campaign may end and the brand is what remains.

Marketing may convince a prospective client to do business with you. Your brand will, in the end, help determine if he continues to do business with you and become a loyal client.

Perhaps you may not have given much thought to your brand before now. If this is the case, I hope that you now see the importance of taking the time to identify and communicate your brand.

Here are some questions that you can answer to help you define your brand.

- Why did you start your business?
- What service or products do you provide?
- Who are your ideal clients?
- How would your ideal clients describe your company?
- Why do your clients choose you over your competition?
- What are a few words that you can use to describe your company?

Write down your answers to these questions, as well as any other questions and answers that come to your mind. Your answers will help clarify your brand.

Now, take a look at the various marketing channels that you are currently using. Look at your website, your business card, your trucks, magazine ads, direct mail pieces, etc. Do they reflect your brand? Is everything consistent and clearly understood?

Does each piece convey the same message, the same feel and the same colors? If you answered yes to these questions, congratulations! You are doing a great job. If you answered no to any of the questions, now is a great time to make the necessary changes to help solidify your brand.

Narrow in on your target market. Does your brand reflect what you want to communicate with them? Do you want to be known as experienced and traditional, or are you more on the cutting edge? Are you thought of as low cost, high volume service, or high quality, higher cost? Does your brand reflect this?

Remember, you cannot be all things to all people, and your brand should help establish this. Trying to do it all adds confusion and dilutes your brand.

The branding created by a fast food restaurant would not work for the branding of a high end gourmet restaurant. They serve two completely different markets. Yet, they both can be successful as long as they are meeting the needs of their customers and have a clear brand. In the proceeding chapters, we will be taking a look at optimizing your web site, social media and various other advertising channels. As we do, keep your brand in mind and how it relates to the message that you want to consistently communicate.

CHAPTER 2
Direct Mail: Friend or Foe?

Before we enter the world of cyberspace and look at bringing in more clients with internet marketing, it's of great importance that we first discuss direct mail.

It is often the case, with new technology being thrown at us every day at a rate like never before in history, that we often forget to take a look at marketing methods which are tried and true and still work today. There are many great new resources available to us, but there is also a lot of hype that we need to sort through. As a result, many Landscapers often overlook the power of direct mail. It is often the case that web designers, social media gurus, and internet marketing companies, try to make you believe that direct mail is dead and simply "old generation".

This is simply not the case. Direct mail, when done properly, can bring in new clients to your business as well as reactivate those who have not used your services for some time.

A few weeks ago, Google made a pitch to me, promoting their widely known Adwords Pay-Per-Click internet marking platform. The approach was not made by a flashing banner on a web page or an email, but instead through a direct mail piece. Yes, even Google sees the power of direct mail!

A few years ago, I was talking to a client about some marketing ideas for his business. One of the ideas I shared involved the use of direct mail. Before I could finish my idea, he let me know that he does not like direct mail because it no longer works. His wife smiled and let him know that the reason she had called me to talk with him, was a result of a direct mail piece that she had received from me. I also sent him a lumpy mail piece (I'll discuss this in a moment) that triggered him to call and hire me to do some marketing for his company. I was curious to find out how much business my original investment of $6.82 had generated from the work I had done for his company. I was pleased to see that it was over $50,000.00. I'm glad that I believe in direct mail! He remains a great client and has seen a positive return on the money that he has invested in marketing and growing his business.

One mistake that Landscapers often make is that if they do try direct mail, they only do one mailing. This can easily result in a low, (if any) response, causing them to conclude that direct mail doesn't work. However, there are several elements that go into creating a successful direct mail campaign, and I will cover them now.

- Before beginning a direct mail or any other advertising campaign it's important to do a SWOT analysis. This allows you to evaluate the strengths, weaknesses, opportunities and threats that are involved in a project or business venture. Using the information from the analysis will be a key part

    of helping you plan your marketing campaign.

- Don't just simply create one mailing piece and stop at that. Instead, develop a campaign based on the goal that you want to achieve. Will you be reaching out to your existing clients or is it a campaign designed to bring in new clients? Have clear objectives and specific metrics that you want to reach. Set a clear goal as you begin with the end in mind.

- Develop a marketing calendar that implements each step of the campaign, including all of the steps along the way, from the design of the campaign to the mailing dates.

- Make your piece different. You want to separate yourself from everyone else. Some ways to do this are, sending oversized postcards, personalized  mail, monthly newsletters and lumpy mail. Lumpy mail is dimensional instead of flat, so that it stands out.

It can be something that you add to an envelope or can even be a physical object that you add postage to and mail. You will be surprised at the things that you can mail. I have seen crazy things like a brick and even a toilet seat with postage attached and mailed "as is" without being placed in a box. Now, I'm not suggesting that you mail either of these!

But you can mail things such as a message in a bottle or a treasure chest to bring attention to your mailing. You can find a full assortments of products and ideas here: www.3dMailResults.com

- Add value. Your clients (or prospective clients) want to know what's in it for them. Write copy that effectively provides not merely features, but the benefits that your offer provides.

- Have a call to action. Give them a reason to schedule an appointment now. Offer something unique and add a time limit to encourage them to respond.

- Have an offer that leads them to a landing page on your web site. It needs to be something that would motivate them to take the time to go on-line and do.

    It could be an added special offer or a special guide that they can download.

- Put yourself in your client's shoes. Look at your mailing piece through the eyes of a prospect. What would be your response to seeing this for the first time? Is it professional, credible, as well as warm? Ask your friends, family and staff for their input.

- Do a VIP mailing to your top clients. You can afford to spend more money on each piece as you will not be sending it to the masses. This might be an area that you may want to consider sending a lumpy mail piece or a specially printed greeting card. Be creative.

- When mailing to prospective clients, seriously consider using EDDM – Every Door Direct Mail from the USPS. Postage cost is lower, as you are mailing to your chosen zip code routes with everyone getting one in their mailbox, so there is no need to address each piece or buy a mailing list. In addition, you can focus your marketing efforts on potential clients by selecting a specific radius of your business and can even use demographic data including age range, household income and size to select the routes that you want to include in your mailing. You can get all of the details at their website: www.eddm.usps.com

- After your first mailing, make changes and tweaks. Don't give up after your first mailing. Also remember that repetition helps keep your name in front of your audience.

- Direct mail that is properly planned and executed can be a powerful element of your overall marketing strategy.
  A key to success is to have a plan in place and implement it.

If you need help with the planning, design or mailing of your campaign, I would be glad to help and will be happy to share some of my ideas with you. Simply contact me by email Chris@SuccessLandscapeMarketing.com or click on the "Contact us" button on the top of our home page at http://www.SuccessLandscapeMarketing.com

CHAPTER 3
Harnessing The Power Of The Internet

The internet has drastically altered the way in which information is shared, which has led to a huge impact on the way business is able to be marketed. It provides enormous opportunities for you as a Landscaper to build your business, as well as your brand.

The internet has become interactive and has opened the door for your clients to share their experiences, both positive and also negative. As a result, it is important for you to have a reputation marketing plan in place. We will discuss this more in coming pages.

The internet has also become local. Google processes over 3.5 billion searches every day, and out of those 27% are local. This means that people are searching for specific services and business within their own area.

For example, someone in Atlanta who is looking for a Landscaper might search for "Atlanta Landscaper" instead of just "Landscaper." As a result, all of the information that is relevant to you is displayed.

Here is another encouraging statistic: 82% of local searches are followed by an action such as a phone call, visit to the location, email or a purchase. This tells us that when someone does a local search, the majority of the time, they are ready to take action.

Next we are going to look at how to maximize local listings for your landscaping business.

Google My Business

Google My Business puts your business information on Search, Maps and Google+ so that your clients and prospective clients can easily find you, regardless of the device that they are using.

As a Landscaper wanting to connect with more local clients, these search results are the most valuable ones you can pursue. Getting ranked locally is also a lot easier and less time consuming than attempting to compete with the entire world. Not only that, but focusing on local rankings will also help you reach geo-targeted clients who are more likely to become your clients.

Google My Business is a new dashboard which replaces Google Places for Business and Google+ Local. Google has experimented with both platforms in the past, which has left many business owners feeling confused and frustrated.

The new Google My Business dashboard will eliminate this confusion by allowing you to manage your business information across all of Google's platforms, including Search, Maps, and Google+. It's a one-stop solution that should help you simplify the whole listing management process in the going forward.

Accessing the dashboard is easy. You can do it from the Google My Business platform on your desktop, or you can download the Google My Business App from the App Store on iTunes or on Android Apps on Google Play.

You can get everything set up for your business by visiting the Google My Business website: www.Google.com/business You can also download a copy of "The Landscapers Ultimate Guide to Google My Business" by visiting our web site: www.SuccessLandscapeMarketing.com and choosing the guide from the drop down menu located under "Marketing Resources" in the web site header.

Getting Google+ and Other Reviews

Client reviews can make or break you. When looking for a Landscaper by performing an online search, many potential clients then decide which Landscaper to choose based on their reviews.

Encourage your clients to visit your Google + page and leave a review for you. Google+ provides you with a link that is personalized just for your business. Incorporate it as part of your follow up system and include the link in your thank you email. A simple screen shot can be part of the email showing them where to locate and click the "write a review" button.

In addition, be sure to include the link on all of your business correspondence as well as ads and marketing materials. This is another great way to promote your link and request reviews. You should also generate a QR code which can be scanned with your client's mobile device to be taken directly to your review page. This process is easy and effective.

List your business in directories such as: Bing, Yelp, and Yahoo. Business listings, Foursquare, and all other reviews that are submitted to those sites will be automatically linked to and will show up on your Google+ listing.

Responding to reviews is just as important as receiving them. Feedback is very important and can go both ways.

Respond promptly. This will show your clients that you are paying attention to what they have to say. Thank them for sharing, and show appreciation to them for being a client. If they share anything negative, make an attempt through your response to resolve any existing issues. Show your concern and take care of the problem immediately.

You can also ask your client to leave reviews on your Facebook business page. To do so, they will go to the Reviews section on the left side of the page's timeline. Next, they will click on the gray stars to choose a rating and can then write a review. Ask them to make the review public. Not only will these reviews show up on Facebook, but the search engines will display them in search results for your business.

Our System For Reputation Management

In order to streamline and automate the review process, we have created our Success Review System. Here is how it works. After you have completed a job, an email is automatically sent to your client thanking them for their business. (This can be personalized in any way that you would like.) They are asked to click on a link to leave feedback. When they do, a simple web form appears for them to list their name, click on a 1-5 star rating and leave their review. They hit the send button and are taken to a page with a video from you (or a member of your staff) thanking them for their review, and inviting them to click one of the icons on the right side of their page to leave the review on Google+, Yelp, Facebook or whatever review site that you have chosen. Now here is where the magic takes place! As long as their review is a 4 or 5 star review, they will be taken to the thank you page with the video, with the request to share their review. If the review is 3 stars or below, here is what happens. The next page has a video with you expressing your concern that the service they received did not meet their expectations. They do not receive a request to share their review on the social media sites. Instead, they receive an email saying that you are sorry that you do not meet their expectations and you (or your staff) will be personally following up with them. In addition, you are immediately sent an email, as well as a text (if you like), notifying you that a client is not happy. This allows your company to follow up with them immediately and handle the problem. It also prevents a negative review being made public before you are able to address it.

As part of the system, we design a review page that shows your logo, information about your business, a map, and all of the 4 and 5 star reviews that you have received. This serves as a micro page and is another way for the search engines to display information about your business.

Overall, reviews are a win-win-win for everyone. It provides those searching for your business with valuable information as they read what others have shared about your business. It lets your clients know you truly care about them, and it helps you to make sure that your clients' expectations are being met. It also attracts more prospects as they see your reviews.

The Importance of Citations For Your Business

So what are citations, and why do I need them? These are questions that you may be asking yourself. To me, the first thing that comes to mind when I hear the word citation is a police officer writing me a ticket! Well, in the world of cyberspace, citations are defined as mentions of your business in directories and other websites. They include your business name along with another piece of business information such as your phone number, your address or your website, or a combination of all three. This is referred to as N.A.P. (Name, Address and Phone.) They are a key component in the ranking algorithms in Google and Bing. The more of them that  you have from quality sources, the better your business is likely to rank. All factors being equal, if you have more citations than your competitor, then you will probably rank higher. Citations that are from well- established and credible portals like "Superpages.com," help increase the degree of certainty that the search engines have about the contact information and categorization of your business. Citations can also be found on local Chamber of Commerce pages, or on a local business association page that includes your business information. They are valuable for you as a local Landscaper as they validate that your business is part of a community. It's hard for someone to fake membership in a Chamber of Commerce, or a city or county business index, or being written about in a local online newspaper or a popular blog. It's important to be sure that your name, address and phone number are consistent across all of your citations. If you have moved or changed your phone number, the wrong information may be still showing. It's important that it is correct, because citations and links form these websites and can dramatically improve your local search engine rankings. If you have more than one listing for a single physical location in an online directory, these other listings are considered duplicates. A variety of negative outcomes can arise from having duplicate listings, detracting from your local business's ability to rank well and win clients. Google makes this clear about the number of listings that you can have, and their guidelines can be found by doing a search for "Guidelines for representing your business on Google."

Now, it's time to make sure that your listings are showing up, and that all of the information is correct.

To start off, be sure to claim your listing on Google, Bing, and Yahoo. Next, claim your listing on the top sources for Landscapers as listed below. After you have done that, search for other directories that will benefit your business. Be sure to find local directories and websites to add your listing to as well.

Here are the top 10 citation sources for Landscapers:

- yellowpages.com
- homeadvisor.com
- superpages.com
- manta.com
- bbb.org
- thumbtack.com
- yelp.com
- local.yahoo.com
- angieslist.com
- dexknows.com

Tips to follow to maximize your citations:

- Establish the NAP format. Be sure to correct listings that are not accurate.
- When you register a new account on a directory site, use the email that matches your business domain.
- Establish your service area.
- Use QR codes when possible.
- When descriptions can be added, be sure to make it appealing to your potential clients. Make sure it is well written and inviting.
- Include photos and videos whenever you have the option. Showcase your business and services and include video testimonials when you can.
- List your real address, do not use a P.O. Box, Fed-EX, UPS, or other box address.

- Be sure to adhere to Google's terms and conditions.
- Use your local phone number in your listing. Do not use an 800 or a tracking number.
- Make sure you are properly listed on webpages and directories of organizations that you are a member of. Make sure the web link works correctly.
- Find local blogs and websites to be listed on.

"Sorry about missing that stop sign. I was updating my blog."

Optimizing Your Web Site

In order to get the most benefit from your web site, you need to make sure that it is fully and properly optimized. The main ways to optimize a website are: Have fresh, relevant and original content on your site. Personalize it. Include copy that also ties in your community. Use videos whenever possible. Be sure to make updates to your Blog on a regular, consistent basis. The search engines love fresh content which contains the information that searchers are looking for.

- Include back links. These are simply other sites that are pointing to your web site. When Google or one of the other search engines looks at your website (they call it crawling the web), and sees that your site has other reputable websites (authority sites), with links that are pointing to your website, they see your site as important, and as a result, it will often rank higher up in the search rankings. The other important key is for your site to link to high-ranking authority sites like CNN, YouTube, etc. When the search engines see that your site is pointing to some of these other high ranking sites that have great information it helps to move your site up in the rankings.

- Use keywords effectively. Keywords are the exact words that your clients are typing in to find what they are looking for. Single keywords are too broad of a search term for local searches. Three to Five words together are known as "long tail keyword phrases." These are much more powerful for local searches since they usually include a geographic identifier. These are usually used for very specific searches and have higher conversions. Optimizing your website with long tail keywords is very important.  Placing 4 to 6 long tail keywords in your pages can help boost your website's rankings. An example of a single keyword would be the term "Landscaper." An example of a long tail keyword would be "Landscaper that builds retaining walls in Dallas." As a result, the person using these words in their search will find specific results for the Landscapers in Dallas who build retaining walls. When someone does a web search, they are often looking for specific information. A single keyword will display broad results, while long tailed keywords will display results that are less general and are more specific.

- When creating content for Facebook, Twitter, blogs, YouTube, etc. always use your keywords in the title first. Content creation with relevant keywords will help your website's organic ranking. Be sure to avoid overstuffing. Overstuffing is excessive use of keywords and is not favored by search engines. In addition, your content will not flow freely and will not sound natural when you overuse keywords. A helpful tip is to read your copy out loud. Does it flow? Does it sound natural? If not, make the necessary changes.

- A great way to find out the best keywords to use for your website or content is by using Google's free keyword tool. You can research your specific keywords and it will make suggestions of keyword terms that are closely related to your search terms. The keyword planner will show you how many searches each term gets per month. This can help you identify the best terms to use, so that the most people will see your information. It will also show you which keywords are rated low, medium or are highly competitive. This is important because it will be easier to rank for the low to medium competition keywords.

- Be sure to add your keywords to your web site. This will help your page rank well in search results. By doing this, you are telling the search engines what your page is all about.

These are the areas of your web site to add them to:

a. Your page title.
b. The header.
c. The Sub Header
d. The Meta description.
e. The body of your paragraphs.

Your Complete Website Checklist

Follow this checklist to get your web site reaching its full potential.

Domain Name and URL's

The domain name is part of the identity of your business. The URL chosen can have a significant impact on brand identity and in a lesser extent, keyword ranking performance. However, how your site domain name and page URLs function can have a significant impact on the crawlability of the site, as well as overall visitor and traffic performance.

__ Short and memorable

__ Uses Keywords

__ Used in email addresses

__ Uses a Favicon

__ Site.com redirects to www version

__ Alternate Domain redirects

__ Home page redirects to root

__ No underscores in filenames

__ Keywords in directory names

__ Multiple pages per directory

__ Registered for 5+ years

__ Multiple versions: .com, .org, .net and .biz

__ Hyphenations

__ Misspellings

__ Product names

__ Brand names

__ Type-in keywords URLs

Site Logo

The logo lends directly to brand identity and site identification.

Note: Time out for a moment while I jump on my soap box. Please treat your logo with respect! Here's what I mean, the colors of your logo and the shape of your logo is not to be changed from media to media. I'm amazed at how many times I have seen a logo look one way on a website, another way on the Facebook business page and then another way on a business card! If the color your graphic artist chose for the background was, for example, PMS 2259 cp, then don't change it. (PMS stands for Pantone Matching System and is a proprietary color space.) Make sure that you have a high resolution version of your logo for print use and a web version for on line use. Your graphic artist can help you with this.

Now, time to continue with the checklist.

__ Displays business name clearly

__ Isn't hidden among clutter

__ Links to home page

__ Unique and original

___ Use tagline consistently across site

Design Considerations

The site design is essentially the first impression that someone gets when they land on your site. You may have all your usability and SEO elements in place, but if the design is lacking then your visitor's impression of you will be lacking as well. A visually appealing site can not only bolster trust and credibility, but it can also make you stand out among other less-appealing sites in your industry.

___ Instant site identification

___ Crisp, clean image quality

___ Clean, clutter-less design

___ Consistent colors and type

___ Whitespace usage

___ Minimal distractions

___ Targets intended audience

___ Easy to navigate

___ Descriptive links

___ Good on-page organization

__ Easy to find phone number

__ Does not use flash

__ Consistent page formatting

__ No or minimal on-page styling

__ Avoid text in images

__ Font size is adequate

__ Font type is friendly

__ Paragraphs not too wide

__ Visual cues to important elements

__ Good overall contrast

__ Low usage of animated graphics

__ Uses obvious action objects

__ Minimize the use of graphics

__ Understandable graphic file names

__ No horizontal scrolling

__ Non-busy background

__ Recognizable look and feel

__ Proper image / text padding

__ Uses trust symbols

__ Works on variety of resolutions

__ Is mobile responsive

Architectural Issues

Website architecture can make or break the performance of a website in the search engines. Poor architectural implementation can create numerous stumbling blocks, if not outright roadblocks, to the search engines as they attempt to crawl your website. On the other hand, a well-implemented foundation can assist both visitors and search engines as they navigate through your website, therefore increasing your site's overall performance.

__ Correct robots.txt file

__ Declare doctype in HTML

__ Validate HTML

__ Don't use frames

__ Alt tag usage on images

__ Custom 404 error page

__ Printer friendly

__ Underlined links

__ Differing link text color

__ Breadcrumb usage

__ Nofollow cart links

__ Robots.txt non-user pages

__ Nofollow non-important links

__ Review no-index usage

__ Validate CSS

__ Check broken links

__ No graphics for ON/YES, etc.

__ Page size less than 50K

__ Flat directory structure

__ Proper site hierarchy

__ Unique titles on all pages

__ Title reflects page info and heading

__ Unique descriptions on pages

__ No long-tail page descriptions

__ Proper bulleted list formats

__ Branded titles

__ No code bloat

__ Minimal use of tables

__ Nav uses absolute links

__ Good anchor text

__ Text can be resized

__ Key concepts are emphasized

__ CSS less browsing

__ Image-less browsing

__ Summarize all tables

Navigation

A strong, user-friendly and search engine friendly navigation is essential in helping people and bots through your site. Your visitors need to find information quickly with minimal hunting, and the search engines need to be able to follow the navigation to reach all site pages with the fewest number of jumps (clicks) necessary. If the navigation is broken or doesn't get people (or search engines) where they need to go, the performance of a site will suffer.

__ Located top

__ Consistent throughout site

__ Links to Home page

__ Links to Contact Us page

__ Links to About Us page

__ Simple to use

__ Indicates current page

__ Links to all main sections

__ Proper categorical divisions

__ Non-clickable is obvious

__ Accurate description text

__ Links to Login

__ Provides Logout link

__ Uses Alt attribute in images

__ No new window links

__ Do not rely on rollovers

__ Avoid cascading menus

__ Targets expert and novice users

__ Absolute links

Content

Content is an essential part of the persuasion process. Pretty, image-based sites may be appealing to the eye, but it's the content that activates trust and appeals to the emotional and logical centers of the brain. The inclusion of content as well as having copy that is effective are all crucially important to the sales process. The ideal situation is to have a site that looks great and is full of helpful content that your potential clients are looking for to help them with their landscaping needs.

__ Grabs visitor attention process

__ Exposes need

__ Demonstrates importance

__ Ties need to benefits

__ Justifies and calls to action

__ Reading level is appropriate

__ Client focused

__ Benefits and features

__ Targets personas

__ Provides reassurances

__ Consistent voice

__ Eliminate superfluous text

__ Reduce/explain industry jargon

__ No typo, spelling or grammar errors

__ Contains internal contextual links

__ Links out to authoritative sources

__ Enhancing keyword usage (SEO)

__ Web version of PDF docs available

__ Consistent use of phrasing

__ No unsubstantiated statements

Content Appearance

Great content can get lost if it's not easy to read or thrown into an otherwise cluttered page. Ensuring that your content fits visually into the site is just as important as having good content to begin with. If you want the sales message to get across, your visitors will need to read it.

__ Short paragraphs

__ Uses sub-headings

__ Uses bulleted lists

__ Calls to action on all pages

__ Good contrast

__ No overly small text for body

__ No overly small text for headings

__ Skim-able and scan-able

__ Keep link options in close proximity

Links and Buttons

Links and calls to action are a great way to allow visitors to navigate from page to page, finding the information that is important to lead them to take the next step. Without these calls to action, many visitors will simply not know what they are expected to do next.

__ Limit the number of links on a page

__ Avoid small buttons and tiny text for links

__ Leave space between links and buttons

__ Avoid using images as the only link

__ Link important commands

__ Underline all links

__ Accurately reflects the page it refers

Home Page

The home page is often the single largest entry-point. It is the page that gives the visitor the sense of who you are and what they can expect.

__ No splash page

__ Instant page identification

__ No Flash

__ Provides overview of site

__ Site purpose is clear

__ Robot meta: NOODP, NOYDIR

About Us Page

Studies have shown that conversion rates for visitors who have visited the About Us page increase measurably. Those who visit here are looking for a few extra elements of trust that will help them decide whether to continue or to move on. What they find can mean the difference in a conversion or the visitor leaving your site for a competitor's.

__ Adequately describes your business

__ Shows team biographies

__ Shows mission statement

__ Up to date information

__ Note associations, certifications and awards

__ Links to support pages

__ Contact page

__ Business news

__ Registration info

__ Job opportunities

__ Newsletters

__ Links to social media profiles

Contact Us Page

Those who land on this page are showing clear intent in wanting to get in touch with you. Providing only a few ways to contact you can alienate visitors who have a particular preference. Providing robust contact options and information ensures that you capture as many would-be clients as possible.

__ Easy to find

__ Multiple contact options:

__ Phone

__ Fax

__ Email

__ Form

__ Chat

__ Client feedback

__ Street map

__ Hours of operation

__ Final call to action

__ Multiple points of contact:

__ Client service

__ Inquiries

__ General info

__ Job applications

__ Billing

__ Management team

__ Ad-free

__ Form requires only essential info

Services Pages

Each service page has a very singular focus. Its job is to provide the visitor with information about the service they need and to convince them that it is exactly what they are looking for. If your service pages cannot convince visitors to call, they will leave your site.

__ Visible calls to action

__ Clear contact info (phone #)

__ Consistent layout

__ Clear service presentation

__ Use photographs ("Before" and "afters" are great!)

__ Guarantee info

__ Service description

__ Client reviews

__ Clutter-free page

__ Service Area

Help and FAQ Pages

Why this is important: if your clients are digging through your help and FAQ pages, chances are they are close to making a decision to purchase and they just need a little extra push.

Make a list of the most commonly asked questions about your landscaping services and include the questions and your answers in your Q & A section. Also think of the questions that your clients should ask and list those along with your answers.

__ Avoid marketing hype

__ Link to additional resources

__ Client support

__ Q & A

Privacy And Security Pages

While most visitors won't read Privacy and Security pages, they do provide necessary assurances that visitors look for in terms of being able to trust you. However, when visitors do click into these pages, certain information needs to be presented to them in order to ensure their needs are met.

__ Present info in easy to read format

__ Provide section summaries

__ Identify information types collected

__ Explain how cookies are used

__ Explain how user information will be used

__ Explain how info will be protected

__ Link to these pages in footer

__ Provide links to contact info

Site Map

Site maps provide a one-click path to any destination within the site and a way for the search engines to quickly find and index all site pages.

Ensuring that your site maps function properly is an important part of ensuring that your visitors can find what they want quickly and that all site pages get properly indexed.

__ Keep information current

__ Link to site map in footer

__ Linked from help and 404 pages

__ Provide overview paragraph

__ Provide intro to main sections

__ Visible site hierarchy

__ Descriptive text and link

__ Link to xml sit

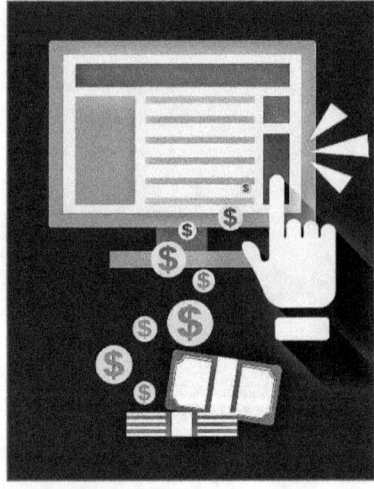

Pay Per Click Advertising

Pay Per Click (PPC) is Advertising on Google (or on another search engine) that places your ads in front of potential clients who are actively searching for a term or "keyword" related to your Landscaping services.

You are charged each time someone clicks on your ad. When a person clicks on your ad, it takes him or her to the landing page that you have set up.

Let's look at an example of a Landscaper in Asheville. They want their ads to show up in front of potential clients, let's say, people who are actively searching for information about "Outdoor kitchens."

The top ads relating to this will show up on the top of the search page. Of course, there is no guarantee that your ad will be clicked, but having a great headline and body content will improve the chances that it will.

The 7 Steps to Set Up a Winning Adwords Campaign

#1 - Set Your Goals

You will want to determine exactly what you're looking to achieve with your campaign. Do you want a specific number of leads per month? Are you looking to increase inbound phone calls, book more appointments, or sign up potential clients for a workshop that you are offering?

#2 - Do Keyword Research

Research the Keywords – Use keyword tools, like Google's Keyword Planner, to find the most relevant keywords people are typing into the search engines to find your Landscaping services.

Research Your Competition – You will want to spend some time looking at the competition to see who consistently is ranking at or near the top of the rankings (you can use a spy tool like Keyword Spy Tool to help). Pay attention to their ad copy and offers. Visit their websites. Sign up for their mailing lists.

Research Your Audience – Where are people talking about,

and reviewing other Landscapers like you, online? Take a look at the reviews they are posting. What do they love/hate about your competition? What are the needs or desires they're looking to fulfill? While doing this part of the research, you should be on the lookout for ideas that you can use in your ad.

#3 The Landing Page/Offer

When your ad is clicked on, it is important that it takes them to the specific area of service that they are looking for. In our example above, the viewer should be taken to a specific page on your website (landing page) that gives him or her detailed information about your outdoor kitchens. It should never take a person to your home page where one can get lost and frustrated, trying to find the information they need. Include photographs, testimonials, and a video on the page. It should be easy to read and have a clear call to action, so the reader knows the next steps to take in scheduling an appointment with you.

Make your ad stand out from the top competitors whom you saw when you were doing your research. Separate yourself from them. It is amazing what just a small improvement over the competition here can make.

#4 Use Exact Match Keywords

When first starting out with AdWords, you will want your keyword list very small (5 – 10 keywords). They are the very specific keywords for the service that you will be advertising. Add all these keywords to your campaign as exact match keywords. As a result, your ads will only be shown when someone types that exact term into the search engine. By doing this, your ads will only show up for the most relevant searches. They will not show up for variations that Google may think are relevant, but are not.

Over time, you can eliminate the keywords that aren't getting clicks/conversions and expand on the ones that are. Your ad words dashboard will provide you with all of this information.

#5 Add Negative Keywords to Your Campaign

Negative keywords are an important part of your campaign as they help to make sure that your ads will only appear to people searching for the Landscaping services that you offer.

Negative keywords help to streamline your ad, presenting it on more relevant search result pages. They can help you reach the most interested clients, reduce your costs, and increase your return on investment (ROI). When you add terms as negative keywords (available for "Search Network only," "Search Network with Display Select," and "Search & Display Networks" campaigns) or as keyword exclusions (for "Display Network only" campaigns), your ad won't show to people searching for those terms or visiting sites that contain those terms.

With negative keywords you can:

- Prevent your ad from showing to people searching for or visiting websites about things you don't offer.
- Show your ads to people who are more likely to click them.
- Reduce costs by excluding keywords where you might be spending money but not getting a return.

When you select negative keywords, you'll want to choose search terms that are similar to your keywords, but signal that people are looking for a different product.

For a Landscaping business, words like "classes" and "courses" may be appropriate to add as negatives, as they indicate Landscaping education, not services.

You can find good negatives by using:

• Your knowledge of the Landscaping industry

• Google's keyword tool

• Third-party keyword tools

• Search Query Performance Reports

Search Query Performance Reports can be obtained directly in the AdWords interface, and they reveal actual search queries where a searcher clicked your ads. You can easily identify any queries irrelevant to your service, and quickly add them as negative keywords to your account to decrease advertising costs and increase conversion rates.

#6 Use Unique and Proven Ads

The ad copy should be highly relevant to the keywords they show up for, and include the exact terms whenever possible. Make sure you stand out from the competition by using different offers, benefits, etc. Your landing page/offer should also reflect the same messaging as your ads. This will help your potential clients feel they are in the right place. If your landing page is not consistent with your ad copy it will hurt your conversions.

Test your ads. To do this you will place at least 2 ads in each ad group and then split test them. As a general rule of thumb, after each ad has at least 30 clicks, delete the lower performing ad and replace it with a new one.

#7 Make Your Ad Mobile Friendly

Be sure to use mobile-preferred ads within your enhanced campaigns. This will promote a customized message with a mobile specific CTA – Call to Action that speaks directly to your mobile users. Combine this with a mobile-optimized landing page. This will result in higher conversion rates and a positive user experience.

#8 Continually Test and Track Your Results

Review the goals that you set for your campaign and track the results. Use AdWords conversion tracking.

Plan various tests to try to maximize your outcome. These tests need to span each step of your campaign, beginning with identification of keywords to bid on and which ad copy to use, to the design of the landing page and any follow-up email marketing campaigns. It is important to run only one test at a time and change one thing at a time. Make a change such as changing your landing page design and then track the results.

Do not change your landing page and also add a set of 15 new keywords to your campaign. If you change both at the same time, you will not know which change made the biggest impact on your results.

Continue to test, test, test! It's possible to know what your potential clients will see as an ad that is appealing and trustworthy to cause them to click on it. You will also find that changing one single word can make a big difference.

So, create variations of your ads and monitor to see which gets the best click through rate, the lowest cost per click, the highest number of conversions, etc. Once you know what works, keep only those ads that are performing well -- and start the process over again.

#9 Mine the Data

You can get data from AdWords that you cannot get anywhere else. Take advantage of it.

You can use the keyword data to find keywords that are good candidates for Search Engine Optimization (SEO) for your website.

As mentioned above, test different messages, headlines and offers in your ads. When you find ones that people really respond to, test them on your landing pages and in other marketing media.

The information that you are provided with from your AdWords campaigns can be used to help you with your entire marketing campaign.

CHAPTER 4
Social Media Strategies
Facebook, Twitter, YouTube and More

I was in a meeting some years ago, when I was told that Facebook was simply a fad which would soon be gone. "Remember My Space?" asked the speaker. In 2012, an article in the Huffington Post, stated that the results of an Associated Press-CNBC poll said that half of Americans think that Facebook is just a passing fad. Fad or not, it had 1.49 billion monthly active users as of 7/28/15, and it should not be overlooked for reaching out to your prospects and clients.

We will also take a look at two other social media channels. Twitter and YouTube. Twitter has over 310 million monthly users and YouTube has one billion each month.

As you can see by the numbers, these platforms provide channels for getting information in front of multitudes of people. You can identify them and target them locally based on their geographic information, as well as their interests.

Getting Started on Twitter

- Select Your User Name

    When creating your account at www.twitter.com you will need to select your user name, referred to on Twitter as your "handle." It is what the public sees to identify your business. It can be a maximum of 15 characters, and ideally you want it to be as short as possible. This is especially helpful with retweets.
    Twitter handles are becoming more difficult to find just like top level domain names are. However, take your time and look for various names that will work for you. Make sure that the name you choose looks trustworthy. Try to match your username as closely as possible to your business name.

- Complete Your Profile.

    This is an important step in creating your brand. An incomplete profile, or one that has a vague description, does not project a professional image. Include a photo that is professional as well. This isn't the place for a selfie!

    Twitter lets you include links in your profile, so use this space strategically. Include your name in your profile so people can recognize you easily. Also, list professional details in your bio, share your location as well as links to your web site.

Use the header photo space for maximum impact for your Twitter account. You can list your expertise and services in the same frame. This way, whenever a user visits your profile they can quickly see all of the important information about you.

- Find Out What Your Clients Are Thinking.

    It's important to be tuned into what is currently happening with your community. Go to www.search.twitter.com and start by searching your own city or town. You can broaden your search by entering the type of healthcare that you provide and the city that your business is located in. You will discover this is the place that conversations are happening about their world every second of the day. This is a big asset as it allows you to enter the conversation that is going on with your clients. This tool should become an important element in the marketing of your business as you are able to specifically find out what your prospects and clients are thinking.

- Follow your clients on Twitter as well as others that you desire to follow.

As a result, they will often follow you in return.

- Post Interesting, Valuable content.

The more that you post, the more you will gain followers. Add photographs and videos to your tweets. Consider mentioning others by their Twitter username (preceded by the @ sign) in your Tweets. This can help you come up with ideas of what to write, it will draw more viewers to your message, and it can even lead to the start of a new conversation.

- Connect With People in Your Niche.

Once you begin to develop a list of followers, find people in your industry with whom to connect. Log into Twitter Analytics and click the Followers tab. Take a look at whom your followers follow, to see people who may be in your niche.

In addition to Twitter Analytics, you can use tools like www.Klout.com and www.Kred.com to find like-minded people on Twitter. Identify people to connect within your niche. Another tool that helps you find like-minded people from a huge category list is www.NearbyTweets.com. It returns Tweets in real time. It is very intuitive, and in addition to being good for finding people to follow, it is a great tool for monitoring the conversation around a particular topic on a local level.

After you identify people of interest, follow them. Don't just retweet their tweets randomly. Keep a close watch on the content which they are sharing. Read their tweets and share your opinions. You may not hear back from them right away, but once they recognize you're adding value, they will start responding.

Another way to connect with influencers is to tag them in your tweets. You might ask a question or appreciate something they've said. By doing this, you acknowledge their industry expertise and get on their radar.

- Discover the Best Times to Tweet

    There are many factors that go into determining the best time to tweet. Fortunately, there are many tools that help you come up with the best times to Tweet. One great example is www.tweriod.com. This tool lets you run an analysis on your own Tweets as well as those of your followers so that you can see when you should Tweet more often.

Another tool is www.FollowerWonk.com. With it, you can dig deeper into your Twitter analytics and discover who your followers are, where are they located, and when do they tweet. It also helps you connect with new influencers in your niche.

- Take Part in Twitter Chats

    Twitter chats are one of the best ways to connect with other Twitter users. You can either organize your own chat or participate in one. There are tools to help you find the most relevant Twitter chats. One tool is www.TweetReports.com. They provide a free Twitter chat schedule, and you can narrow the list to just the chats that are available at a specific time.

    You also can register your own Twitter chats on the website. Fill out the form with all of the required information about your chat. Once it's listed, anyone can see it and join.

    After scheduling your chat, you need to get prepared for it. A tool like www.TweetChat helps you conduct your chat sessions. All tweets with the designated hashtag appear on your screen. You can reply, retweet, or view the entire conversion from this platform, so there's no need to go back to Twitter.

Always try to add value to Twitter chats, whether you're hosting them or not. If you're planning to host a chat, spread the word on various social networks. Ask your friends to participate and give them a reason to join in.

Organize chats once a month and Twitter users will soon start taking notice of you.

- Use Automated Services Wisely

It's nice to be greeted, but Twitter users are smart enough to know if a welcome message is automated or personalized. Automated Twitter messaging can be a great tool if you use it correctly. Start with a clever question that can't be ignored. But remember that you're asking a question, and some users will probably answer it. So, check your inbox frequently to continue the conversation.

#10 : Include Your Twitter URL in Your Author Bio

Is your Twitter profile included in your author profile and other social profiles? If you don't link to your Twitter profile in articles you've written, you'll likely miss out on many new followers and mentions.

Adding your Twitter URL is an easy way to guide users to your Twitter profile. Include your Twitter profile in your bio. Whenever a user clicks on a link, they're redirected to your Twitter profile.

Be sure to include the Twitter logo in all of your marketing material along with a link when applicable, such as in your email signature, web site, and your other online listings.

It takes time and patience to build your followers, but the more active that you are and the more valuable content that you publish, the quicker it will happen and soon begin to pay off.

Maximizing Facebook For Your Business

The chances are pretty good that you have already established a Facebook business page for your business. So I will not be covering those steps here. Instead, we will jump right into discovering some of the ways in which you can get the maximum benefit from using Facebook as a way to promote your business. However, if you do need guidance on getting set up, be sure to visit: www.FacebookForBusiness. It was created by Facebook to provide step by step instructions to help you get started and provide you with resources. In addition, it contains a plethora of useful information on a variety of topics. So, even if you are already established on Facebook, check it out, as it is a valuable resource.

On the next page we will take a look at 7 tips that will help you get the most out of Facebook for promoting your business.

1. Establish a plan, and list all of the goals that need to be accomplished to create a comprehensive Facebook marketing campaign. Schedule action steps on your calendar, and carry out these steps on a continual basis.

2. Make sure that you have an attractive cover photo that coordinates with your brand. The header should be clear, easy to read, and incorporate the same look, feel and design elements that make up your website, marketing materials, business card, letterhead, signage etc.

   This is a good time to pause for a moment and take a mental inventory of all of the items that I just listed. Or better yet, if they are available now, take a physical look. Do they all reflect a level of professionalism? Are they all coordinated and carry your brand throughout? In cases of printed pieces, are they professionally printed and not simply Xerox copies? If not, make the necessary changes.

If you need any help with your branding, drop me a note and I will be glad to give you some tips. Chris@SuccessLandscapeMarketing.com.
Now, back to Facebook!

3. In our Twitter discussion, we talked about the importance of completely filling out your profile. The same applies to Facebook. Take the time to make sure that your listing is complete and accurate. Verify all of the information that appears under the "About" tab . Go into the Page Info and make sure everything is complete and includes your hours, both the short and long business description, website, etc. Make sure it is well written and reflects your brand.

4. Just as we discussed the importance of keeping your blog and website up to date with fresh, relevant content, the same should be applied to your Facebook page. Your page should not look like an abandoned ghost town that has not been updated in some time.

   Here is an ideal way to add fresh content. When you publish a new post to your blog, share it on your Facebook page. Be sure to include a link from your Facebook page that leads back to the article on your website. This also gives you motivation to make sure that you are publishing fresh content to your blog. Like I shared earlier, develop a strategy to make sure that it happens and stick to it!

Make sure that you are sharing tips, articles and resources that your readers have an interest in. Not sales copy that says, "Buy now, buy now!"

The fresher the content, the more you will engage people. A good rule of thumb is to share interesting content 80% of the time and sales content about 20% of the time. Now your sales content should of course be interesting, but my point is not to use your Facebook page mainly as a sales platform.

Facebook is looking to see if your fans either:

a.)   Like your post.

b.)   Comment on your post.

c.)   Share your post, or

d.)   Click a link that you have included in your post.

To be effective, your post needs to motivate a viewer to do one of the above when they see your post. Otherwise, they will not show your posts in their newsfeed, and as a result your reach will decline.

When your post does cause a reader to take one of the actions, it not only helps by showing this post in your news feed, but as other posts consistently attract engagement, your reach is strengthened. As a result, when you do share posts that are promotional, those posts will also get more reach and show up in the news feed, because you have established that fans are interested in the post that you are sharing. Facebook, just like Google, will reward you when their users are engaging with your content.

Some ways to generate engagement is to post a question that sparks nostalgia or just a really good feeling. When you do, expect to  see your post likes accelerate. For example, post a photo of a beautiful sunset. Say something like, "I just love sunsets, don't you?" Another way is to include an image of a quote that is sure to bring likes. You can also ask for a like. Include a photo and the caption "LIKE if you….." Do the same with the same caption and a funny photo…test them and see which one brings the best response.

You can increase the engagement on your post when they are encouraged to join the conversation. Everyone loves to give their opinion, so ask questions that they will answer while providing you with valuable information.
To generate more shares, make the post worthy of sharing and make sure that it has an image that instantly tells your fans what the post is about. Something like: "See how your back yard can be transformed from an eye sore to a place of beauty."

Think of the services that you offer and how you can share them in fun, creative ways.
Quotes are often shared as well. The key for sharing is using ones that are meaningful to your audience.
To generate posts that will cause your viewers to click a link, include an image that grabs their attention.
A post that creates a bit of curiosity is a great strategy to get the link clicked. Tease them with the content; don't give it all away in the post so that they feel compelled to click to find out more.

5. Create an Effective Face Book Ad Campaign.
   Facebook ads can be highly profitable for your business and can be implemented without breaking

the bank. Let's take a look at the best ways to create your campaign.

a.) Use Audience Insights For Target Data

You can mine your audience by using audience insights in your Facebook platform to locate new potential clients to target, based on the characteristics and interests of people who already like your page.

First, click on Audience Insights in the Ad Manager.
Use Audience Insights to target your ads.
In the pop-up window, select People Connected to Your Page.
Next, click on People Connected to Your Page.
You will now see your Audience Insights.
Demographics is the default on the horizontal menu.
When you get to Audience Insights, you'll see your demographics.

Scroll down the page until you see a drop-down menu on the bottom left of the page that says People Connected To. Although you are using Audience Insights for your page, you still need to select your page name in that field. Select your page name under People Connected To.

You will now see a variety of metrics, including age

and gender distribution among your current page likes, lifestyle, relationship status, education level and job title.

Use what you know about your audience demographics to create targeted audiences for your Facebook ads.

Based on the insights Facebook provides, put together new target audiences to split test against or add to your current audiences. Use what you know about your audience demographics to create meaningful, directed ads.

b.) Align Your Ad With the Campaign Landing Page

The content of the Facebook post should be aligned with the content of the landing page for two reasons.

First, you will get a higher Ad Relevance score, and as a result, you'll pay less per click. Over the last couple of years, Facebook ads have become more competitive and consequently more expensive, so it makes a lot of sense to do this.

Second, alignment among ads and landing pages increases your conversion rate. Once people click the ad, they expect to get exactly what the post promised. If they do, your website and brand gain credibility, and potential clients are more likely to trust your business as a whole. This is the same strategy that we discussed earlier about landing pages. They should always contain relevant information that lines up completely with what your audience is looking for.

In most cases, you probably will not be offering something to a client that requires them to purchase on-line, but if you decide to do so, establishing trust is critical. Trust is always important, but is particularly important if you are running Facebook ads to increase sales of a product or service, because clients are more willing to insert their payment information and complete the purchase if the brand looks trustworthy. Plus, a high degree of alignment among the ads and landing pages typically lowers shopping cart drop-off rates and increases conversion rates.

c.) Test One Ad Element at a Time

The strategy here is the same that we covered in the section on using Adwords. Instead of creating different ads and split testing them, create variations of whichever ad currently performs best, and change one element at a time.
For example, take your best ad, make copies of it and change the headline of each version. You now have multiple ads that are identical except for the

headline that you can test.

Take your best Facebook ad and duplicate it, except for the headline, to see which gets the best response.

After you determine which ad gets the best response, make copies of it and test another element like description or image.

Remember, also test combinations of different split tests. For example, take the winning headline and put it with various descriptions to determine the winning description. Now put the winning description with one of the other tested headlines to see how it does. You never know, it might even outperform the winning headline/description combination.

Once you determine your most effective ad, test each element separately to see if that gets an even better response.

d.) Experiment With Different Ad Placements

Instead of just choosing news feed right-column ads or going for all news feed ads, split test the different ad placements. If you have one campaign with news feed right-column ads, as well as desktop and mobile ads, run a placement report to find out how they perform.

Ideally, you would have three campaigns or ad sets: One for news feed right-column ads, one for news feed desktop ads, and one for news feed mobile ads. This allows you to control the budget to a much higher degree than if all ad formats were in one campaign or ad set.

e.) Target New People With Like Campaigns

When you set up a like campaign with the Power Editor or in the live Facebook account, you are allowed to exclude audiences such as people who already like your page.
Here's how.
Login and click Create Ad in the top right corner. You then see the regular campaign setup. Next, scroll down to Connections. Click Add a Connection Type and choose Facebook Pages. Then select the last option, Exclude People Who Like Your Page.

Go to the Connections section to exclude people who already like your page.
It is a common best practice to exclude people who already like your page, because the whole point of the campaign is to get additional likes, not to get irrelevant impressions by showing your ads to those people who already like your page.

f.) Refine Targeting with Conversion Audiences

If you have installed the remarketing pixel, you can exclude people who already converted to prevent irrelevant impressions and clicks.

Go to your campaign settings and edit the Targeting & Placement section.

Edit the Targeting & Placement section to exclude people who already converted from your ads.

A window will pop up to allow you to edit your ad set. Click in the Custom Audiences field.

Click in the Custom Audiences field in the Targeting tab.

Once you click, the word "Include" will appear. Click the arrow next to "Include" to open up the drop-down menu. Select Exclude.

Facebook will automatically provide audiences to choose from for this field, such as Exclude People Who Like [your page name]. After you select this custom audience to exclude from your targeting, double-check the change in the overview of the settings.

After you exclude a custom audience, double-check your settings.

g.) Use Geographic (GEO) Targeting

To save money on bidding, set up ad sets according to geographic target areas. Ideally, each ad set should just target one geographic area because the cost per click can vary greatly.

By separating different geographic targets from the start, you can adjust your bids accordingly. Bid higher where it makes sense, and use other geographic areas on a seasonal basis or exclude them entirely.

A key factor to keep in mind is that ad sets can also target cities or zip codes. This is powerful! Armed with the information that we covered, you can generate a powerful campaign that is to your ideal client.

6. **Using YouTube to Market Your Business**

Although YouTube may not be thought of as a social media platform, it actually is, because you can have subscribers, send messages, and leave comments. So it really does become a social media platform. It is certainly a powerful platform with around 4 billion video views every day, and 1 billion users.

After Google, it is also the number two place that people go for online searches.

Getting Started – To get started using YouTube, you will first need to create your channel. This step may require a little time, but the effort you put into creating and customizing the channel to suit your business will be well worth it. When you customize your channel, you should include your logo and customize the colors to those related to your logo and your business. This will give your channel a customized look and help it be recognized by those familiar with your brand, like we discussed in earlier chapters. During the initial setup phase, you should include the option of allowing users to subscribe to your channel. This will ensure that your target market is receiving your latest videos.

Types of Videos – The best types of videos for you to create are those that are educationally covering Landscaping issues, and those that answer FAQ's. Whenever you answer questions that people want know, it increases the video ranking. These types of videos will allow you to educate your subscribers about your business and establish you as an authority. Think out of the box and come up with other creative videos that you can produce. It's best if you can appear in each video, but if you are limited with time constraints, delegate a special segment that appears, one day a week, in which an outgoing member of your team relays valuable information. Another idea is "Tuesday Testimonials" in which you could feature one of your clients showing off a Landscaping service that you have created for them.

Sharing – When you create your YouTube channel, you will then be able to share your videos across your other social media pages. Posting your videos on your Facebook page is a great way to show your clients that you are on YouTube, and that your videos have something to offer. You can also share links to your videos in your tweets, which will help expand your subscribers to your YouTube channel.

Feedback – Each time that you post a new video, you can gain valuable feedback. Your clients will be able to leave comments about your video, products, or tips that you included in your video. This is a great way for you to see what is working and what you may need to change.

Online Visibility – YouTube is also a great way for Landscapers to increase their online visibility. When someone searches for a product or service that you offer or have mentioned in a video, your link will be presented in those search results. A search for "Ideas for outdoor landscaping" has several videos including one with over 700,000 views.

Be sure to include relevant keywords in your video titles. This will help increase the visibility of your videos and gain valuable exposure for your business. Simply title it with the information of how people will search for it.

Another important way to title your video is to include a GEO tag for local search results. If you are a Landscaper in Altanta, one of your videos may be "Atlanta Landscaper shows amazing before and after backyard transformation." As you can see in the title, we have included the GEO identifier (Atlanta) , the keyword "Landscaper" and the description of the content. You will also want to put in tags so that it gets peoples' attention and can possibly show up in the search engines.

SearchEngineWatch.com is an excellent resource for anything related to SEO and web optimization topics. Brian Dean published an excellent article; "*5 Advanced YouTube SEO Tactics to Drive More Traffic to Your Videos & Website*" on the site last year. Let's take a look at Brian's tips to generate more traffic. Be sure to check out the entire article for more useful information.

Tips to Generate More Traffic to Your Videos

a.) Write Super-Long Video Descriptions.

YouTube, Google and the other search engines are not able to watch or listen to your videos. As a result, they rely heavily on the text surrounding your video to understand the topic of your video. That is why it is important to include as much information as possible to the description area of your video. Doing so will help your video rank for your target keyword as well as the long tail keywords that are used in the description.

b.) Optimize Around "Video Keywords"

Keywords that are called "Video Keywords" tend to have video results on Google's first page. To determine the best keyword for your video, do a search and see if there are video results on the first page of Google. If there are, then that is a keyword that you should strongly consider because you can potentially get your video ranked in Google and YouTube.

c.) Encourage Viewers to Subscribe and Like

YouTube's algorithm does not use back links so it puts a major amount of weight on user experience signals. If people enjoy watching your video, expect it to crush it in YouTube search. Subscribing and liking are two of the most important user experience signals that YouTube uses. When someone likes your video enough to subscribe after watching it, it sends a strong message to YouTube that you have a winning video on your hands. Likes are much less important, but they still count. You can ramp up both of these user experience signals by asking. At the end of your video, give people a strong call to action that encourages them to subscribe.

d.) Get More Views From Online Communities

Online communities such as LinkedIn groups are fantastic places to funnel traffic from.

It is important to first establish trust by being involved in the community. Don't just pop in and drop links to your content everywhere.

Look at the questions being asked and answer them as you participate in the group.

Because the number and quality of your video views is one of the most important YouTube ranking factors, getting views from targeted communities is a big asset for you. Just find a question in the community that your video could help answer. Then provide some value and suggest that people watch your video if they want more information. As you freely share your videos in online communities, you will generate the quality, high-retention views that YouTube likes to see.

e.) Create Keyword-Rich Playlists

As your video collection begins to grow, you will want to make sure that you keep it organized. When you have about ten videos on your YouTube channel, organize them into tightly themed playlists. This is one of the easiest ways to get YouTube search traffic to your videos.

Make sure that your play list is keyword rich which will give YouTube the needed information about the topic of the video. Just like we saw with the importance of a long description, the more text base content that you add will generate more views.

To create your videos, you can use an inexpensive video camera or even your iPhone. The video quality is an important element, but so is the sound quality. In fact, viewers will endure a less than average picture quality that has excellent sound, but will not like a video that has a great picture but bad sound. Use an external microphone that can be plugged directly into your video camera or phone. Of course, the goal is to have both great audio and video quality.

Another important element is to have good lighting for your videos. You may have heard that the eyes are the windows to the soul and they should be well lit. If the lights are too high and in the wrong position overhead, it will give you dark bags under the eyes. This is referred to as raccoon eyes and can be corrected by lowering the lights.
Check out YouTube for tips on the best equipment and ways to use it for your videos.

Another option is to create a video that shows a presentation. This is accomplished by using PowerPoint for Windows or Keynote for Mac.

Videos are very search engine friendly and can rank on the first page rather quickly, using the techniques that we discussed. YouTube is the biggest video sharing site, but it is not the only video sharing site. You should also add your videos to other video sharing sites like Vimeo, Viddler, Kewego, and more. You can simply do a Google search for video sharing sites, and you'll get an entire list of all the places that you can post videos.

As we wrap up this chapter, we have discussed Facebook, Twitter and YouTube. I encourage you also to develop a presence on Linkedin and look into other social sites that might be beneficial to your business. It is much more important to start off on a few social media sites. Begin to participate and add valuable content. Then add other sites as you are able. A mistake that is often made is to sign up for many sites, but then get overwhelmed. This often results in a lack of your participation. A Facebook page, for example, that has 37 followers and the last post with a date from months ago, does not instill much confidence in either your clients or potential clients that view your page. In a situation like that, it would be better to not even have a Facebook presence.

"He is a Creature of the Web! He must log on and check his email to survive!"

CHAPTER 5
Developing an Email Marketing Strategy

Implementing an email strategy as a part of your overall marketing plan is an effective way to stay in touch with your clients and increase overall traffic to your website, as well as your business.

If you do not already have an email marketing program, then a good place to start is with Aweber or Constant Contact. If you are looking for the ultimate platform, then I highly recommend Infusionsoft. We use it in our agency and also to manage campaigns for some of our clients that are also on the Infusionsoft platform. It is very powerful and does have a steep learning curve, so if you would like more information, drop me a note: Chris@SuccessLandscapeMarketing.com. I will be happy to share my thoughts and give you more information. Regardless of the program or software that you invest in, the important thing is to learn it, fully use it, and reap the benefits that are possible by implementing a complete email marketing campaign. A few years ago, Kate Kieger Lee published an excellent article on Forbes.com with 15 email marketing tips. Below is a combination of her tips and mine.

1. **Make your sign up area prominent.**

Post a signup form on your homepage, blog, Facebook page, and wherever else your clients and fans are already active. You might want to collect special dates and anniversaries of your clients. This can be done as part of the email sign up process or added to their record at any point. I suggest that although it takes a slight bit of manual labor to add it yourself, it is more important to have as few fields as possible when collecting email addresses. First and Last name, along with their email address, is really all that you need.

As I mentioned earlier, give them an incentive to sign up.

2. **Let your subscribers know what to expect.** Whether you plan to send a newsletter, weekly tips, links to your weekly videos, etc., it's important they know what to expect and how often to expect it. Give them as much information as possible on your signup form, so they can decide whether or not they want to be on the list.

3. **Send a welcome email.** Thank them for being part of your community, and let them know that you have some special things in store for them. You might even send new subscribers a special offer exclusive content, as your way of thanking them for their loyalty.

4. **Carry out your brand in your newsletter design**.
Your email campaigns should match your brand's look and feel. If you're using a template, be sure to customize it to include your company's colors and logo in the header. If your emails are consistent with the rest of your company's content, then readers will feel more familiar from the start.

5. **Have a neat, clean and easy to read design**.
Your subscribers are busy people who get a lot of email, so it's safe to assume you don't have their undivided attention. Instead of one long block, break up your content into short paragraphs. Include subheadings and images to guide readers through your email, making it easier to read. Be sure to use a catchy subject line that entices your reader to open it. Test your subject lines to see which ones give you the best open rate. Also, consider adding a teaser to the top of your newsletter to tell subscribers what's in store. Placing this at the top of the header will cause it to show to the right of the sender's name before they open the email. So, if they are quickly scanning their unopened emails, this line in your email can be the extra piece it takes to get them to open it. If you are sending an email newsletter, use photographs with stories next to each one. Include a portion of the story with a link to "read more" to take them to your blog for the complete article. An effective strategy is to end the sentence at a

chosen point that will add curiosity so they will wish to "read more."

6. **Send valuable content**. Send material that is of interest to them. Email providers, such as those mentioned earlier, allow you to segment your list into various groups so that you can send content that is relevant to the people reading it. If you're sending different emails for different groups, then you can ask subscribers to check a box to join a particular group on your signup form.

    Infusionsoft creates tag for different groups and lets you begin a campaign to follow up with them based on their particular interest. An example would be that you might create a report on how your Landscaping services can help add value to their home. When they sign up to receive the report, a tag is added to their account such as "Landscape guide" sent. Then you can have a campaign in place to automatically send out additional information over time, such as articles and videos that you have created showing your work. Sending relevant content will keep your readers engaged, and engaged readers will look forward to your newsletter and share it with friends.

7. **Keep a publishing calendar**. A regular newsletter is a commitment. If you go several months without sending anything, then your subscribers will forget

about you, and they'll be more likely to delete the next email, or worse, mark it as spam. Make time to plan, write, design, and send your newsletters regularly.

Include your newsletter in your overall marketing campaign and calendar.

8. **Proofread and edit your content**. Have an editor read your material and make the necessary corrections. It is often not as easy for the writer to catch their mistakes. Another helpful tip is to ready the copy out loud. This helps you catch mistakes and get an idea of the overall composition of your words.

Even editors need editors. When you're working on your publishing calendar, leave plenty of time for the editing and revision process. Once you send a campaign, it goes straight to the inbox, and you can't go back and update it. Email and Newsletters contain meaningful content, and sloppy ones reflect poorly on your business. Grammar and style are just as important for email as they are for your website, blog and other marketing materials.

9. **Test before sending.** Different email clients and mobile devices display emails differently. Send test emails to colleagues, or use a testing

program to make sure your emails are going to look good on screens which are both big and small. Testing reveals design mistakes before it is too late. Email software can usually predict whether or not a campaign will get caught in a spam filter. You could even set up accounts with a few different email services for easy testing. Avoid sending one big image as a campaign, and cover your bases with a plain-text option for every email.

10. **Check to make sure that it is mobile friendly.** If a campaign doesn't show up on mobile devices, it's not going to perform very well. Everything you send should be mobile-friendly. Consumers have said that they would either close or delete an email that's not optimized for mobile. Be sure to choose a template that is mobile responsive.

11. **Avoid SPAM.** It is important that you know your spam rules. A lot of innocent people have sent spam because they didn't know any better. Read up on the CAN-SPAM act to avoid any trouble. Put simply, you're allowed to send bulk email only to people who specifically asked to be on your mailing list. If you collected email addresses for a lunch giveaway or an event invitation, then you don't have permission to send marketing emails unless you made that clear at signup. Be sure to include an obvious unsubscribe link in every email and don't forget to remind subscribers how they got on

your list in the first place.

12. **Make it easy to share**. Send content that people want to share, and make it easy for them to do it. Sure, subscribers can forward your campaign to friends, but that's a lot to ask. Include a public link to the web version of your campaign so people can read it outside of their email programs, and consider adding Twitter and Facebook links to your newsletter, so readers can share your content where they're already active. When their friends start sharing and subscribing, you'll know it's working.

13. **Be aware of your stats**. Most email newsletter services offer free reports that contain helpful information. Learn how to read and understand your reports, so you can use the stats to improve your campaigns going forward. Pay attention to your open and click rates, and identify any patterns that make those numbers go up or down. If a campaign receives a high number of unsubscribes, see if you can determine the cause and make the necessary adjustments.

14. **Be warm and friendly**. You can still be professional while having a warm tone in your email newsletters. Since most emails come directly from one person, people expect human voices in their inboxes. There's a good chance your subscribers

are already in an informal frame of mind when they're checking their email, so an overly formal or stodgy voice might seem out of place. Plus, they've given you their email address, so you're already on a first-name basis. If you collect first names on your signup form, you can dynamically include them in your email greetings.

15. **Only send email if you have something to say.** This one seems obvious, but too many will start email newsletters with no plan and nothing to say. Email is simply a way to publish content—the content itself has to come first. Before starting a newsletter, make sure it's a sustainable commitment that will help you achieve your business goals. Otherwise, you'll be wasting your subscribers' time and your own time. Ask yourself: What's the goal for this kind of communication? What do we have to say? How will we measure success? Send thoughtful newsletters, and keep the focus on the message of your business.

All of the different email marketing terms can be a bit confusing. So to give you a clear picture as we conclude this chapter, here is a list from autosend.io of the top 50 email terms. They are important for you to know, in order for you to successfully learn email marketing.

Email Marketing Dictionary

A

Acceptable Spam Report Rate – The rate at which you can be reported as SPAM without harming your sender reputation. Anything over 0.1% (1 report per 1000 emails) will get a warning.

Acceptance Rate – The percentage of email messages that are accepted by the mail server. Just because an email is accepted by the mail server does not mean it will get to an inbox.

Autoresponder – Triggered emails, personalization, dynamic content, and other tools that send emails or add content to emails on a one-to-one or one-to-some basis without manual intervention according to rules established by a brand.

B

Blacklist – A list that denotes IP addresses as spammer IPs, impeding email deliverability.

Behavior-Based Email – A message sent to an individual subscriber in response to an action taken by that person (e.g., cart abandoned) or because of the arrival of an event indicated by the subscriber (e.g., their birthday); also known as trigger-based emails.

Bounce Rate – The rate at which your emails are not delivered. There are two types of bounces, hard and soft, both of which are defined later in this glossary. An acceptable bounce rate is less than 5%.

Bulk Mail – Large scale email marketing sends in which the same content goes to a large group of people.

C

CAN-SPAM – Short for 'Controlling the Assault of Non-Solicited Pornography And Marketing Act of 2003,' it's a law that outlines rules for commercial email, establishes requirements for commercial messages, provides email recipients with the right to make you stop emailing them, and lays out consequences for violations of the Act. You can read more about compliance in our post about marketing laws.

Clicks Per Delivered – A percentage measure of the number of clicks divided by the number of emails delivered to the intended inbox.

Clicks Per Open – A percentage measure of the number of clicks divided by the number of opens.

CPM (Cost Per Thousand) – In email marketing, CPM commonly refers to the cost per 1000 names on a given rental list. For example, a rental list priced at $250 CPM would mean that the list owner charges $.25 per email address. We'll get into buying lists later in this post.

CTR (Click-Through Rate) – The percentage (the number of unique clicks divided by the number that were opened) of recipients that click on a given URL in your email.

Conversion Rate – The percentage of recipients who respond to your call-to-action in an email marketing campaign or promotion. This is one measure of your email campaign's success.

D

Dedicated IP – In email marketing, it refers to an IP address from which only you send email.

Digest Email – An email that is automatically generated by an electronic mailing list and which combines all exchanged emails during a time period (e.g. day, week, month, etc.) or when a volume limit is reached (e.g. every 10 or 100 messages) into one single message.

Double Opt-In – The recommended method of building an email list, it requires subscribers to confirm their opt- in by clicking a link in a confirmation email or responding to the confirmation email in some other way.

E

Email Campaign – An email or series of lead nurturing emails designed to accomplish an overall marketing goal.

Email Click Through Rate – A way of measuring the success of an email campaign by the number of users that clicked on a specific link.

Email Filter – A technique used to block email based on the sender, subject line, or content of an email.

Email Marketing – Directly marketing a commercial message to a group of people using email. In its broadest sense, every email sent to a potential or current customer could be considered email marketing.

Email Marketing ROI – A metric used to measure the overall effectiveness of a marketing campaign to help marketers make better decisions about allocating future investments.

Email Marketing Open Rate – Percentage of subscribers who opened an email.

Email Sponsorships – Buying ad space in an email newsletter or sponsoring a specific article or series of articles. Advertisers pay to have their ad inserted into the body of the email.

F

False Positive – A false positive occurs when a legitimate

permission-based email is incorrectly filtered or blocked as spam.

H

Hard Bounce – A hard bounce is the failed delivery of an email due to a permanent reason like a non-existent, invalid, or blocked email address.

Honey Pot – A planted email address by organizations trying to combat spam that, when a spammer harvests and emails, identifies that sender as a spammer.

House List (or Retention List) – One of your most valuable marketing assets, it's a permission-based list that you built yourself with opt-in subscribers.

HTML Email – Sending HTML email makes it possible to get creative with the design of your emails.

I

IP Warmup – Sending a progressively increasing number of emails out of an IP address in order to build the IP's reputation.

L

Landing Page – A lead-capture page on your website that is linked to from an email to provide additional information directly related to products or services promoted in the email's call-to-action.

Levels of Authentication – A way of establishing a sender's identity, and ensure the sender is allowed to send from a given domain.

List Segmentation – Selecting a target audience or group of individuals for whom your email message is relevant. A segmented list means a more targeted and relevant email campaign, thus a higher response rate and less unsubscribes and spam reports.

O

Open Rate – The percentage of emails opened in an email marketing campaign, or the percentage opened of the total number of emails sent.

Opt-In (or Subscribe) – To opt-in or subscribe to an email list is to choose to receive email communications by supplying your email address to a particular company, website or individual, thereby giving them permission to email you. The subscriber can often indicate areas of personal interest (e.g. mountain biking) and/or indicate what types of emails they wish to receive from the sender (e.g. newsletters).

Opt-Out (or Unsubscribe) – When a subscriber chooses not to receive email communications from the sender anymore, and requests removal from your email list. It is legally required that you provide a clear way to opt out in every email you send.

P

Personalization – Adding elements to your email that are personalized based on information you already know about them. It could refer to addressing the recipient by name, referencing past purchases, or other content unique to each recipient.

Physical Address – The physical, street address of the company sending the email, usually found in the footer of an email. Its inclusion is a legal requirement for all email marketing.

Plain Text Email – An email sent without HTML. You should always give your recipients the option to read emails in either HTML or plain text for better readability.

Privacy Policy – A clear description of a website or company's policy on the use of information collected from and about website visitors and what they do, and do not do, with the data.

R

Read or Open Length – A measure of the length of time a person opens the email until they close it.

Rental List (or Acquisition List) – Not a recommended email marketing technique. It is a list of clients or a targeted group of recipients who have opted in to receive information about certain subjects, usually targeted by something like interest, profession, or demographic information.

S

Sender Score – A free service of Return Path. It's a reputation rating from 0-100 for every outgoing mail server IP address. Mail servers will check your Sender Score before deciding what to do with your emails. A score of over 90 is good.

Shared IP – A less costly option than a dedicated IP address, it is an IP address from which many people send emails.

Signature File – A tagline or short block of text at the end of an email message that identifies the sender and provides additional information such as company name, physical address, and contact information.

Single Opt-In – A single opt-in list is created when users sign up for email communications, but don't confirm the action. This means they can be signed up for a list by someone else, and as such is not a recommended way to build a healthy email marketing list.

Soft Bounce – A soft bounce is the failed delivery of an email due to a temporary issue, like a full mailbox or an unavailable server.

Spam or UCE (Unsolicited Commercial Email) – Email sent to someone who has not opted-in or given permission to email to the sender. Over 90% of email sent is classified as spam.

Spam Cop – A paid spam service that plants their own emails, and monitors who harvests the address and spams it.

Spam Trap – An email address that was once valid, but no longer is. If you email this address, you'll receive a hard bounce notice. When the mail server sees consistent traffic going to the dead email, however, they can turn the email into a spam trap. It will stop returning a hard bounce for the known bad address, and instead, accept the message and report the sender as a spammer.

SPF – Short for 'Sender Policy Framework', it's a DNS record that says on whose behalf an IP or domain sends email.

T

Transactional Email – A message sent to an individual subscriber in response to that person making a transaction, such as a purchase (e.g., order confirmation emails, shipping notification emails, etc.) or an administrative request (e.g., password reset email, email address change confirmation email, etc.)

W

Welcome Email – A message automatically sent to a new subscriber just after they've opted in, that welcomes them to your email program and seeks further engagement.

Whitelist – Instead of listing IP addresses to block, awhitelist includes IP addresses that have been approved to deliver email to a recipient.

Win-Back Email – A message sent to an individual subscriber in response to that person having not engaged with your emails or having made a purchase in a long time, in an effort to get them to engage and make a purchase.

Chapter 6
Staying on Top of Landscaping Trends

Continually learning about new products and trends in Landscaping will not only help you remain cutting edge, (no pun intended!) but it provides you with great material to share with your potential and current clients.

I recently attended "The Landscape Show" here in Orlando. It was a great event with over 7,000 industry professionals attending and over 800 booth spaces. The exhibitors provided a wealth of products and knowledge and the workshops that were offered did the same.

One of my favorite speakers was Debbie Mola Mickler. Debbie is part of the Walt Disney World Horticulture team. She did an excellent presentation on current trends and shared that a trend can also be known as a "unique profit maker". I love that! Thinking this way immediately moves you from the mindset of "Oh, here we go again, another fad!" to thinking about how you can incorporate this into your business. (Remember what I shared in Chapter 4 about that "fad" called Facebook!?)

So, how do you learn about the latest trends? One really effective way is to listen to what new things your clients are asking you for.

It is vitally important to educate your team to treat these questions as valuable information that can be a win-win for everyone. Look for patterns. Are you getting several requests for a new product or service? TV shows and magazines keep your clients informed with landscaping ideas so be prepared to consider their request. Take a serious look and determine if this is something that you can incorporate into your business.

Industry events are another excellent resource to stay on top of new products and trends. Keep an open mind when attending these events and reading industry publications.

One of my clients that specializes in hardscaping is attending the Hardscape North America conference. They will be competing in the HNA Installer Championship. This will provide them with excellent material that they can share in their marketing materials, blog, etc.

The internet, social media and blogs are other great places to visit to see new trends and what people are interested in.

Once you decide to offer a new product or service, be sure to share it on your website, blog, social media and in your newsletter. Be sure to take before and after pictures. These are always a big hit and will in vision your clients about what you can do for them.

Be sure to visit my blog for new landscaping ideas, reports and news on what is currently trending and how to market it. www.SuccessLandscapeMarketing.com

Chapter 7
Next Steps: Developing Your Plan of Action

Congratulations, you have made it through the book!

Your next step is to take action and get results! Time and time again I have seen entrepreneurs get excited about implementing marketing ideas in their businesses, but they soon become overwhelmed, or are held back by paralysis of analysis.

I want to encourage you to take action, so that your business will profit from what you have learned in this book.

Begin by implementing one of the strategies, and build from there. It's important to make a total commitment to do so, or it will never happen. Feel free to drop me an email with any questions that you may have: Chris@SuccessLandscapeMarketing.com.

If you find yourself with enough already on your plate and unable to implement a complete marketing strategy for your business, I understand completely. You became a Landscaping professional to help people and meet their Landscaping needs. That is where your time is best spent. Not trying to figure out the latest Google changes or other mysteries of marketing. You have the Landscaping expertise to provide lots of services that people need, and with the proper marketing expertise you will be able to reach even more.

What are you currently doing to ensure that more people know about your Landscaping services today than yesterday?

If you don't have a consistent marketing plan in place, with more people learning about your Landscaping services, you're not developing a pipeline of potential new clients. This means that you are going to see fewer clients in the future as a result.

That sounds pretty obvious, but I am always surprised when I talk to Landscapers and ask them about their promotional efforts.

When I look at the pipeline-filling activities of most Landscapers, I see mostly a haphazard approach. Often it is just a campaign here and there (if any), with only a vague idea of a strategy. As a result, they have no idea as to whether they are getting a positive return on their investment. No wonder so many businesses become skeptical of marketing.

Very rarely do I see coordinated, systematic metrics driven efforts to reach a wider audience that brings in more business.

But, this kind of focused, ongoing and intentional approach is exactly what is needed to predictably grow your Landscaping business.

I would love to talk to you and provide a complimentary analysis, detailing where you currently stand, and the potential that can be achieved. My goal is to bring you more clients, more referrals, and more revenue.

Regardless of which action step you decide to take, I'm here for you, and can be contacted by email:
Chris@SuccessLandscapeMarketing.com
Web: www.SuccessLandscapeMarketing.com

Thanks for reading…and here's to your Success!

> *"A goal without a plan is just a wish."*
> — Antoine de Saint-Exupér

www.ingramcontent.com/pod-product-compliance
Lightning Source LLC
Chambersburg PA
CBHW060354190526
45169CB00002B/588